Table of Contents

Tons of Turtles

Turtles and Tortoises

Laura Marsh

NATIONAL GEOGRAPHIC

Washington, D.C.

For the Denmark School in Denmark, ME – L. F. M.

This British English edition published in 2017 by Collins, an imprint of HarperCollins*Publishers*, The News Building, 1 London Bridge Street, London. SE1 9GF.

Browse the complete Collins catalogue at
www.collins.co.uk

A catalogue record for this publication is available from the British Library.

ISBN: 978-0-00-826666-0
US Edition ISBN: 978-1-4263-2293-8

Editor: Shelby Alinsky
Art Director: Amanda Larsen
Editorial: Snapdragon Books
Designer: YAY! Design
Photo Editor: Christina Ascani
Rights Clearance Specialists: Michael Cassady & Mari Robinson
Manufacturing Manager: Rachel Faulise

The publisher and author gratefully acknowledge the expert content review of this book by Frank Slavens, retired curator of reptiles, Woodland Park Zoo, and the literacy review of this book by Mariam Jean Dreher, professor of reading education, University of Maryland, College Park.

Printed in China by RR Donnelley APS

The cover features a painted turtle. Many red snapper turtles enjoy the sunshine on page 1. Page 3 shows an Indian star tortoise.

Photo Credits
GI: Getty Images   SS: Shutterstock
NGC: National Geographic Creative
Cover, Donald M. Jones/Minden Pictures; 1, Bob Caddick/Alamy; 3, Eric Isselee/SS; 4-5, Rich Carey/SS; 6 (UP CTR), Raffaella Calzoni/SS; 6 (LO LE), Edwin Butter/SS; 6 (LO RT), Gary Carter/Corbis; 7 (CTR), Joe Cicak/GI; 7 (LO), Nattika/SS; 8, Alex Mustard/NaturePL; 9 (UP), Medford Taylor/NGC; 9 (LO), Jim Abernethy/NGC; 10-11, James Hager/Robert Harding; 12-13, Joe McDonald/Visuals Unlimited; 14 (UP LE), Jonathan Bird/SeaPics.com; 14 (CTR RT), Ger Bosma/Alamy; 14 (LO LE), Scott Camazine/Science Source; 15 (UP RT), Jurgen Freund/NaturePL; 15 (CTR LE), Chris Brignell/FLPA/Biosphoto; 15 (LO RT), Frans Lanting/MINT Images; 16, Mike Quinn/NGC; 17 (UP RT), artcasta/SS; 17 (LO CTR), D. Kucharski K. K/SS; 18, Cheryl Molennor/Alamy; 19 (UP RT), Steve Winter/NGC; 19 (LO LE), Ingo Arndt/Minden Pictures/Corbis; 20, K. Hinze/Corbis; 21 (UP), Claude Thouvenin/Corbis; 21 (LO), Stanislav Halcin/Alamy; 22, Rene van Bakel/ASAblanca/GI; 23, Vetta/GI; 24-25, M Swiet Productions/GI; 26 (CTR RT), Sukpaiboonwat/SS; 26 (LO LE), M. Watson/ARDEA; 27 (UP RT), Marc Shandro/GI; 27 (CTR LE), Cloudia Spinner/SS; 27 (LO RT), Daniel Heuclin/NaturePL; 28 (UP), SA Team/Foto Natura/NGC; 29 (UP LE), Ty Milford/Masterfile/Corbis; 29 (UP RT), Hero Images/GI; 29 (LO), clintspencer/iStockphoto; 30 (LO LE), Rich Carey/SS; 30 (LO RT), Matthew Oldfield Travel Photography/Alamy; 31 (UP LE), ymgerman/SS; 31 (UP RT), Eugene Kalenkovich/SS; 31 (LO LE), Jak Wonderly/NGC; 31 (LO RT), Jak Wonderly/NGC; 32 (UP LE), K. Hinze/Corbis; 32 (UP RT), FloridaStock/SS; 32 (LO LE), NGC; 32 (LO RT), Medford Taylor/NGC; (HEADER THROUGHOUT), Saranyoo Wongchai/SS; (TURTLE TERM THROUGHOUT), h4nk/SS

Oceans and lakes. Deserts and forests. Ponds and streams.

Turtles live in many places. They live all over the world, except in very cold areas.

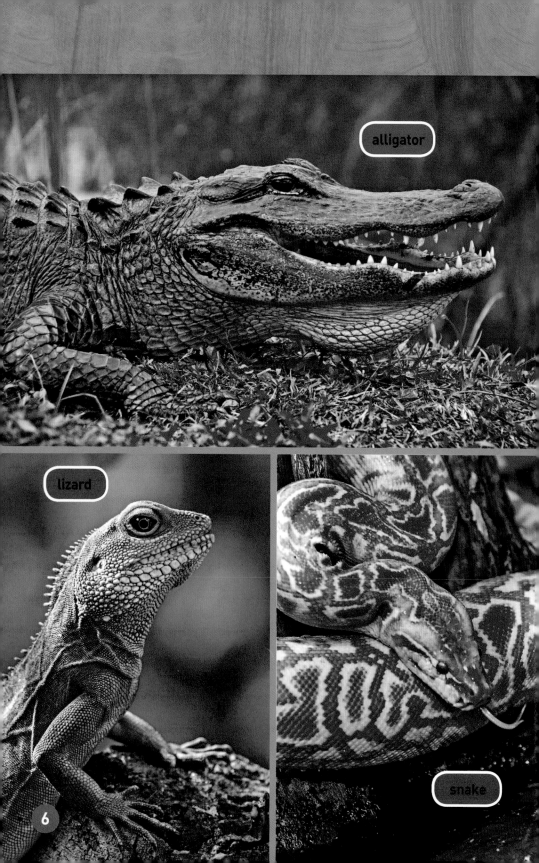

alligator

lizard

snake

Turtles are reptiles. Alligators, lizards, and snakes are reptiles, too. Reptiles have scaly skin. Most reptiles lay eggs.

box turtle

Turtles and Tortoises

loggerhead
musk turtle

There are more than 300 kinds
of turtles. Turtles mainly live in the
water. They have webbed feet or
flippers to help them swim. Their
shells are quite flat.

Q What is a turtle's favourite song?

A "Jingle Shells."

Florida cooter

Turtle Term

WEBBED FEET: Feet with skin between the toes. The skin stretches out to look like a web.

baby green sea turtle

Tortoises live on land.

They do not have webbed feet. They have stumpy legs for walking. Their shells are round and tall.

leopard tortoise

Keeping Safe

Turtles walk slowly. They can't move quickly away from danger. So their bodies help protect them.

BEAK: A turtle's beak can cause a nasty bite. This bite might scare a predator away.

NOSTRILS: A turtle has nostrils near the top of its beak. It can breathe with just the tip of its nose out of water. The rest of its body is hidden underwater.

NECK AND LEGS: Many turtles can pull their neck and legs into their shell when danger is near.

SHELL: Most turtles have a hard shell. It protects the body like a helmet protects your head.

Turtle Term

PREDATOR: An animal that hunts and eats other animals

PROTECT: To keep safe

black-knobbed sawback turtle

SCUTES: Scutes are bony plates that protect some animals. Scutes, like the ones on a turtle's shell, make it harder for a predator to eat the turtle.

6 COOL FACTS
About Turtles and Tortoises

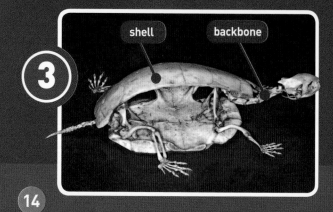

1

Leatherback sea turtles are the largest turtles. They can grow to be over 2 metres long and weigh 900 kilograms.

2

Speckled tortoises are the smallest tortoises. They may grow to be only 6 cm long.

shell   backbone

3

Turtles and tortoises are the only animals that have both a backbone and a shell.

Some turtles make sounds. The strangest sounds come from leatherbacks. When they're nesting, they make burping noises!

4

5

Turtles can see colours. Red, orange, and yellow are colours they seem to like best.

Giant tortoises can live longer than any other turtle or tortoise – more than 100 years. One giant tortoise lived to be 152!

6

Crunch and Munch

It's turtle lunchtime! Lots of foods are on the menu.

A turtle uses its beak to catch, hold, and cut food.

snapping turtle

Some turtles and tortoises only eat plants. Others only eat small animals. Snails, worms, and insects are favourite foods. A few kinds of turtles and tortoises eat both plants and animals.

Tiny Turtles and Tortoises

baby gopher tortoise

Baby turtles and tortoises eat the same kinds of foods that adults eat. Babies can do this as soon as they hatch.

A mother turtle digs a nest in the dirt or sand. She lays her eggs in the nest. Then she covers it.

A Pacific ridley sea turtle lays eggs.

olive ridley sea turtle

EGG TOOTH

red-eared turtle

The eggs sit for many weeks. Then, *tap, tap. Craaaack!* The eggs hatch.

Baby turtles and tortoises have an egg tooth. They use the sharp tooth to break out of their shells.

Turtle Term

EGG TOOTH: A sharp point on a baby turtle or tortoise's beak

western Hermann's tortoise

Once they are out, the tiny babies start to crawl. And they're off!

green sea turtles

Life in the Sea

When baby turtles hatch,
they head for the sea.

leatherback sea turtles

loggerhead turtle

Turtles live in warm
ocean waters all over the
world. They have big flippers.
The flippers help the turtles
swim.

A turtle spends its whole life in the sea. It often travels far.

Male turtles never leave the water. Female turtles only come on land to lay eggs.

green sea turtle

Females return to lay their eggs on the same beaches where they hatched.

25

Terrific Turtles and Tortoises!

Lots of turtles and tortoises are special in their own way.

PIG-NOSED TURTLE
You can tell how this turtle got its name. Look at its nose!

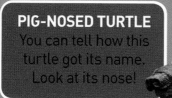

MATA MATA TURTLE
The mata mata looks like a leaf in the stream where it lives.

GALÁPAGOS TORTOISE

The Galápagos tortoise can grow to be more than 1.5 m long. It weighs up to 250 kg. And it eats only plants.

EASTERN LONG-NECKED TURTLE

The neck on this turtle is as long as its shell. It stretches out and grabs passing animals. It can hunt without moving much at all.

ALLIGATOR SNAPPING TURTLE

Part of this huge turtle's tongue looks like a worm. Fish swim toward it. They think it is food. Then, *chomp!* The turtle grabs dinner.

A Helping Hand

leatherback sea turtle

More than half of the world's turtles are in danger of dying out.

Many turtles and tortoises in our world need help. They need open space in the wild. They need clean water. They need people to stop hunting them for food.

How Can You Help Turtles and Tortoises?

1 Enjoy watching turtles in the wild. Don't keep them as pets.

2 Learn as much as you can about turtles and tortoises. Teach others what you learn.

NATIONAL GEOGRAPHIC

Turtles and Tortoises

Laura Marsh

3 Pick up rubbish such as plastic bags and balloons. These look like food to turtles. Turtles can get hurt if they eat the rubbish.

4 If you see a tortoise near a road, ask an adult to help the tortoise cross safely. Always place the tortoise in the same direction it was going.

What in the World?

These pictures are up-close views of things in a turtle's world. Use the hints to work out what's in the pictures. Answers are on page 31.

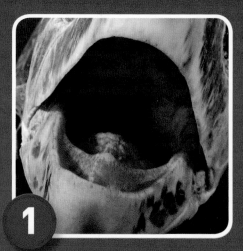

1

HINT: This is the part of a turtle that bites.

2

HINT: Turtles lay these.

Word Bank

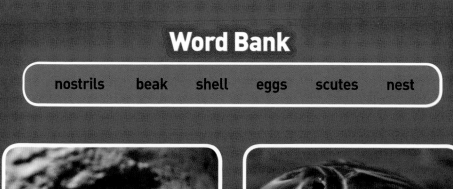

nostrils   beak   shell   eggs   scutes   nest

3

HINT: This place is for eggs.

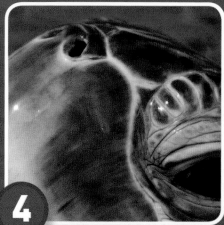

4

HINT: These are near the top of a turtle's beak.

5

HINT: These bony plates make a turtle hard to eat.

6

HINT: This protects a turtle.

EGG TOOTH: A sharp point on a baby baby turtle or tortoise's beak

PREDATOR: An animal that hunts and eats other animals

PROTECT: To keep safe

WEBBED FEET: Feet with skin between the toes. The skin stretches out to look like a web.